Language: English

These materials are designed to assist you in learning about hope. They should not be used for medical advice, counseling, or other health-related services. iFred, The Shine Hope Company, and Kathryn Goetzke do not endorse or provide any medical advice, diagnosis, or treatment. The information provided herein should not be used for the diagnosis or treatment of any medical condition and cannot be substituted for the advice of physicians, licensed professionals, or therapists who are familiar with your specific situation. Consult a licensed medical professional, or call 911, if you are in need of immediate assistance.

ISBN: 978-1-7359395-8-2

© 2020, Kathryn Goetzke.

All rights reserved. No part of this book may be reproduced, shared or distributed without the written permission of the publisher.

For more information, please contact kathryngoetzke@theshinehopecompany.com.

Hopeful Minds

Hopeful Minds is a curriculum developed by Kathryn Goetzke, Founder of the International Foundation for Research and Education on ~~Depression~~ Hope (iFred) and CEO of The Shine Hope Company, alongside a group of hope experts. The program is based on research that suggests hope is a measurable and teachable skill. It impacts all outcomes in life, including academic and athletic performance, health, and resilience. Our aim is to equip children, educators, and parents with the tools they need to create, maintain, and grow hope even during the most trying times.

Our focus is on prevention through practical tools and exercises. It is easily adaptable in different cultures through modifying stories and uses activities and examples to enhance lessons. Hope impacts an individual's ability to address economic challenges, environmental issues, job security, family relationships, and food security, so it is imperative to not underestimate the power of hope.

The program is cyclical, using the sunflower as a continuous symbol for hope. The sunflower is based on the rebranding work by iFred, focusing on universal symbolism to create a 'brand' for hope. Please consider planting sunflower gardens or fields for hope, or creating artworks for hope, to share the message and website so it is easier for people to find their way to our program.

We are using the theory of a growth mindset to start building our future programs to show hope in action, through presentations on the science of hope, stories of Hopeful Heros, and strategies for hope. **We call it the 'how-to' of hope, or hope in action.**

So please stay in touch, through signing up for our newsletter at
theshinehopecompany.com/hopebeat-weekly

We would like to thank the following people for their contribution to our programs:

This program would not be possible without the brilliant leadership, support, and commitment to hope by:

Myron L. Belfer MD, MPA, Harvard Catalyst

Myron is Professor of Psychiatry in the Department of Psychiatry, Children's Hospital Boston, Harvard Medical School, and Senior Associate in Psychiatry at the Children's Hospital of Boston. Dr. Belfer is a Champion for Hope.

Kathryn Goetzke MBA, Author, Creator
Contributors: Taylor Steed, Katharine Lee-Kramer, Veronica O'Brien
Sarah Mellen, Mic Fariscal, Anna Termulo Montances and **Naneth Samoya-Jumawid**

To our advisors, hope contributors, and experts:
Dr. Edward Barksdale, Dr. Frank Gard Jameson, Mayor Hillary Schieve, Kristy L. Stark M.A., Ed.M., BCBA, Karen Kirby PhD, MSc, BSc, C.Psychol, AfBPS, SFHEA, Ulster University, **Marie Dunne and the Northern Ireland** team that helped plant the seeds for this work.

Pioneers in early Hope Science including **Dr. Crystal Bryce, Dr. Dan Tomasulo, Dr. Chan Hellman, Dr. Matthew Gallagher, Dr. Jennifer Cheavens** and the late **Dr. Shane Lopez.**

iFred Board of Directors:
Tom Dean, Susan Minamyer, Jim Link, Dr. John Grohol, Kathryn Goetzke, Dr. Mindy Magrane

The Hopeful Minds Advisory Board

Some of our early funders: Sutter Health, Anthem, The Gordon Family Giving Fund of the Parasol Tahoe Community Foundation, The Shine Hope Company, and The Mood Factory.

IN SPECIAL RECOGNITION
Susan Minamyer, whose unconditional love, support, encouragement, faith, and brilliance planted and watered the seeds necessary to create and grow this program. Kathryn's big brothers **Arnold and Fred, and Clara, Maura, Jack, Sophie, Charles, and Sarah,** who continue to strengthen, build, and inspire Kathryn's hope.

IN HONOR
In recognition of all in the world that were impacted by hopelessness in some way, shape or form, and left us way too early, including a few close to our hearts. Thank you for teaching us so much about life, love, and hope. May we spread Hope far and wide in your name and honor:
Jon and Sally Goetzke, Tom Foorman, Dr. Stephen C. Gleason, Vicky Harrison, Eloise Land, Jesse Lewis, Austin Weirich, Warren Robertson, and **Chase Reel.**

TABLE OF CONTENTS

Introduction to Hopeful Minds 6
   The What and Why of Hope 9
   What is Hope? 9
   Why is Hope Important? 11
   Hopelessness 11
   The Five Keys to Shine Hope™ 13

7 Ways to Shine Hope As a Family 15
   Display Shine Posters Throughout the House 15
   Use the 90-Second Pause 15
   Practice Happiness Habits Together 15
   Write Hope Hero Stories 16
   Write My Shine Hope Stories 16
   Create Family Goals, and Check Progress 17
   Plant Sunflower Gardens for Hope 17

Stress Skills 22
   Allostatic Load 22
   Positive Feelings and Inspired Actions 23
   How to Teach Stress Skills at Home 25

Happiness Habits 27
   How to Teach Happiness Habits at Home 27

Inspired Actions 29
   WOOP 29
   SMART goals 30
   How to Teach Inspired Actions at Home 30

Nourishing Networks 33
   How to Teach Nourishing Networks at Home 33

Eliminating Challenges 36
   How to Teach Eliminating Challenges at Home 38

Resources for Stress, Anxiety, and Depression 44
Additional Resources for Parents 52
Hope Journey: Next Steps 54
Where to Find Support 55

Introduction to Hopeful Minds

Thank you for choosing hope. Hope is a skill each and every person needs to learn, as it impacts all areas of their life. By choosing Hopeful Minds, you are taking the first step towards teaching yourself and your children critical skills that will have lasting, positive impacts on their futures.

Higher hope is associated with higher grades, improved attention in class, reduced likelihood of anxiety and depression, less violence, less likelihood of weapon carrying in school, less likelihood of risky behaviors and addiction, less loneliness, better sports performance, and better quality relationships.

Studies have found that anxiety and depression can begin to appear by age 7 and will continue to develop through middle school and high school. Therefore, the more we can encourage children to aspire to increase their hope, the more we can help them nurture the skills they will need to succeed. You can see the latest science and research on hope at Hopeful Minds: www.theshinehopecompany.com/research

Learning hope starts at home. We can help our children increase their hope through small lifestyle changes. By focusing on using stress skills and happiness habits, and by incorporating hopeful language into your conversations, you can help your children live hopeful, healthy lives.

The most important terms we use in our hope curriculum, and that we hope you will start using with your children, include:

HOPE: We define hope as a vision for the future, fueled by both positive feelings and inspired actions.

HOPELESSNESS: Hopelessness is a feeling of despair and a sense of helplessness. It is both emotional (a negative feeling) and motivational (an inability to act). We proactively manage hopelessness with hope skills.

POSITIVE FEELINGS: Positive feelings are those feelings that help us to stay hopeful as we work towards our goals.

INSPIRED ACTIONS: Inspired actions are the deliberate steps you take away from hopelessness and toward your goals in life.

UPSTAIRS BRAIN: This is where our thinking, imagining, problem-solving, and learning occur. This part of the brain is responsible for the development of sound decision-making and planning, control over emotions and body, and self-understanding and empathy. The upstairs brain is also where we access our positive feelings.

DOWNSTAIRS BRAIN: Also referred to as the reptilian brain, this part of the brain is responsible for basic functions such as breathing, blinking, heart rate, and fight, flight, freeze, or fawn mode. It is also responsible for the chemical stimulus associated with strong emotions, such as anger, sadness, and fear.

STRESS RESPONSE: Your stress response is when an external or internal trigger causes your brain to release stress hormones, such as cortisol, adrenaline, and norepinephrine, that force you into your fight, flight, freeze, or fawn mode.

STRESS SKILLS: These are actions that help you navigate your stress response and work through your body's chemical response to external stimuli.

NOURISHING NETWORKS: Your Nourishing Networks are the Hope Networks of the people in your life that provide you with support, help you stay on track, encourage you to succeed, and who you do the same for in return.

ELIMINATING CHALLENGES: Challenges to Hope are negative habits of thought, like limiting beliefs, automatic negative thoughts, all-or-nothing thinking, negative bias, rumination, worry, focusing on uncontrollables, attaching to outcomes, and internalizing failure, that move us from hope to hopelessness. Eliminating challenges is the conscious act of using hope skills to overcome these challenges to hope and maintain Hope.

THE HOPE MATRIX™: The Hope Matrix is the process that we use to get from hopelessness to hope. The Hope Matrix teaches us that togrow hope, we must move from despair to positive feelings, and from helplessness to inspired actions.

SHINE: This is the mnemonic we use to remember our hope skills. SHINE stands for: **S**tress Skills, **H**appiness Habits, **I**nspired Actions, **N**ourishing Networks, **E**liminating Challenges

THE HOPEFUL MINDS PARENT'S GUIDE AIMS TO:

- Give you, as parents and guardians, a broad understanding of what hope is, why it is important, and how hope impacts all areas of your children's lives.
- Introduce you to our curriculums and inspire you to do the full curriculums at home with your children.
- Provide you, as parents and guardians, with easy ways to discuss and reinforce the Five Keys to Shine Hope at home: Stress Skills, Happiness Habits, Inspired Actions, Nourishing Networks, and Eliminating Challenges.

This program was designed to be used globally, as hope is a universal need. We suggest starting with this guide to familiarize yourself with hope and hope skills. You can then use our other curriculums to further introduce your children to hope in easy-to-understand ways.

Our curriculums are available to download at
www.hopefulminds.org/curriculums

Hopeful Minds Overview 3 Lesson Curriculum
Hopeful Minds Deep Dive 16 Lesson Curriculum
Hopeful Minds Teen Hopeguide

We also have several courses online, that take you deeper into our concepts, including a My Shine Hope Story Course, Hopeful Mindsets Overview, Hopeful Mindsets in the Workplace, Hopeful Mindsets for Veterans, and Educator Training. You can also sign-up for a no cost 5-Day Hope Challenge.

If you would like to be notified when new curriculums become available, or if you have questions or feedback, please reach out to us at activate@theshinehopecompany.com.

The What and Why of Hope

Learning hope starts at home, and small lifestyle changes can help children embrace a hopeful mindset. Teaching hope not only empowers children but also breaks the stigma of discussing challenges, opening the door for meaningful conversations about overcoming challenges.

We believe you play a key role in instilling this essential concept in your children's lives, so get enthusiastic and creative with our suggestions. By reinforcing stress skills, happiness habits, and setting smart goals, you'll not only help your children become more hopeful but also make it easier to manage and support them. Thank you for bringing hope into your home and for helping us teach every child how to create, maintain, and grow hope.

WHAT IS HOPE?

In order to teach hope, we first have to understand what exactly it is. There are many definitions of hope, so we will discuss a few:

Dr. Shane Lopez, a hope expert: "Hope is the feeling you have when you have a goal, are excited about achieving that goal, and then you figure out how you can achieve your goal."

Dr. Dan Tomasulo, author of *Learned Hopefulness*: "Hope is a reorganization of perceptions to foster the belief that you have control in the future."

Dr. Crystal Bryce, Associate Dean of Student Affairs at University of Texas at Tyler - School of Medicine: "Hope to me isn't squishy. Hope is something that we have control over. It is something cognitive. It's a skill. It's something that we can work toward."

Dr. Chan Hellman, Founding Director of the Hope Research Center: "Hope is the belief that the future will be better than today."

Our Founder started from the definition of hopelessness and worked her way towards the definition we use for hope. Ultimately she wanted to figure out - how do we get from hopelessness to hope. She came to the following definition:

HOPE is a vision for something in your future, fueled by both **POSITIVE FEELINGS** and **INSPIRED ACTIONS.**

Positive feelings are feelings that help us stay hopeful as we work towards our goals. Inspired or smart actions are actions that propel us towards our goals.

It is this cycle of positive feelings to smart actions that creates and sustains hope. However, hope is not necessarily something we are born with (or maybe we are, and we unlearn it); it is something we must learn. Just like reading or arithmetic, hope is a teachable skill that must be continually practiced.

Hope and wish are often used interchangeably in the media, which negatively impacts the global understanding of the need for hope. It's time to redefine our understanding of hope because science has taught us one thing for sure: a hope is not a wish. **A hope is both a <u>positive feeling</u> and <u>inspired action</u>.**

To help conceptualize how we move from hopelessness to hope, our Founder developed the Hope Matrix:

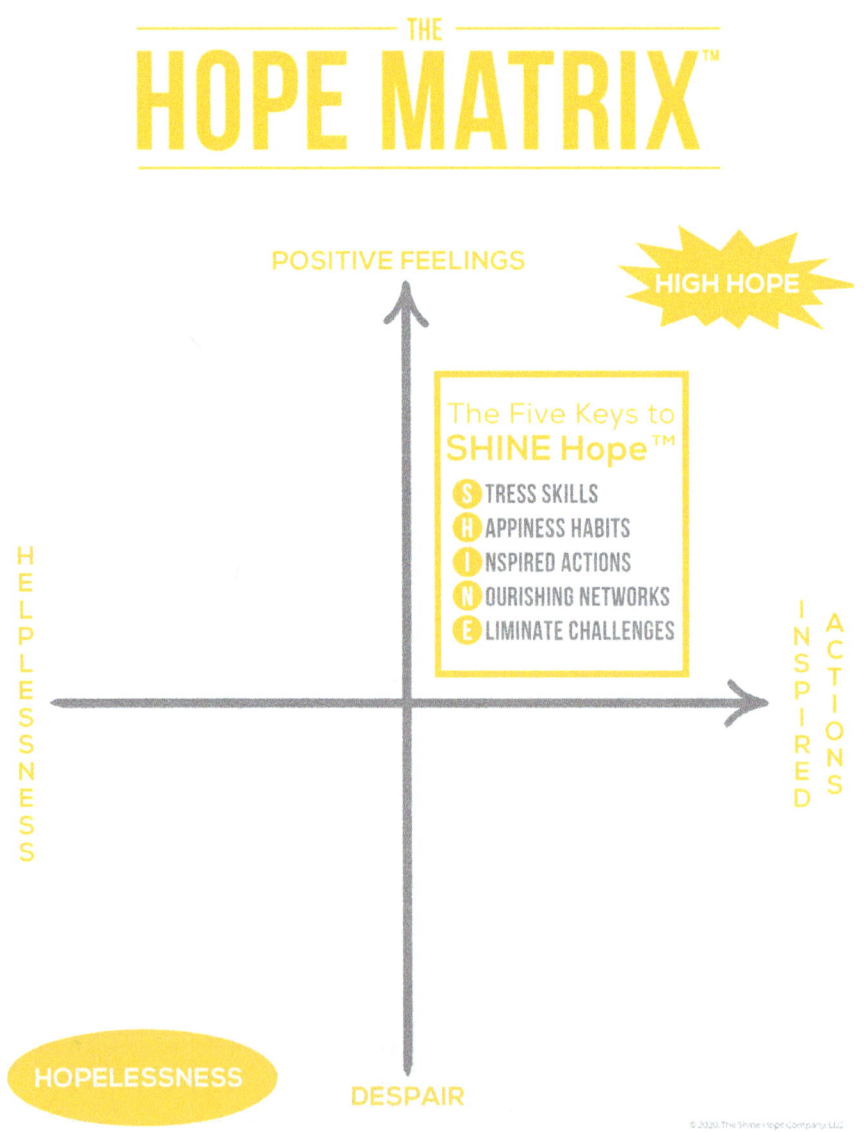

WHY IS HOPE IMPORTANT?

Doctors and scientists have been studying hope for decades because hope is a known protective factor that leads to resilience and success in our lives. Higher hope is associated with better academic performance, less stress, increased productivity, quality leadership, resilience, lower anxiety, better social connection, and less loneliness.

We encourage you to review the extensive amount of research on positive outcomes of increasing hope in your life at: www.theshinehopecompany.com/research/

It is astounding, the power of hope.

HOPELESSNESS

To fully understand the benefits of hope, it is important to understand the other side - hopelessness. Hopelessness is defined as **emotional despair and motivational helplessness.** It is associated with many negative life outcomes, including addictions, risky behaviors, carrying weapons at school, violence, bullying, anxiety, depression, and suicide. Hopelessness is often a consequence of discrimination and is very high in inner-city youth and the LGBTQ community. While we teach each and every child these skills, it is especially important we reach these populations. You can learn about the research surrounding hopelessness at www.theshinehopecompany.com/research/.

HOPELESSNESS is characterized by
EMOTIONAL DESPAIR *(sadness, anger, fear)* and
MOTIVATIONAL HELPLESSNESS *(a sense of powerlessness)*

Hopelessness is the primary symptom of depression, and global statistics have reported that 1 in 4 youth experience clinically elevated depression, and 1 in 5 youth experience clinically elevated anxiety. Hopelessness is also the leading predictor of suicide, which is the number one cause of death, globally, for teen girls.

Hopelessness is also linked to many adverse outcomes including risky behaviors (i.e., substance misuse, reckless driving, violence, weapon carrying, bullying), poor education outcomes (i.e., dropping out, poor grades), poor social connection, and more. By teaching hope skills and the importance of hope, it is our goal to combat hopelessness to lower rates of delinquent and risky behavior, while increasing success and fulfillment for children around the world.

Many children have accumulated Adverse Childhood Experiences (ACEs) by the time they start school – researchers have found more than 60% of adults worldwide have experience at least one type of ACE. ACEs are potentially toxic traumatic events that occur in childhood until the age of 17. These ACE's include events such as experiencing violence, abuse, or neglect; witnessing violence in the home or community; or having a family member attempt or die from suicide.

There are also environmental factors that comprise a child's sense of safety, stability, and bonding, such as growing up around substance misuse, mental health problems, and instability due to parental separation. ACEs increase the likelihood that a child will have physical or mental health issues in adulthood. Children who experience ACEs have a higher rate of chronic health problems, substance abuse, and mental health issues. ACEs can also negatively impact education and job opportunities.

By teaching hope and, as a result, resilience, we are arming our children with tools to combat the negative consequences of these experiences and create positive feelings and inspired action instead. While ACEs are not preventable, hope is a key ingredient to navigating those challenges for positive outcomes.

Understanding the impact of hopelessness helps us reinforce and highlight the importance of building hope within our young generations.

The Five Keys to Shine Hope™

We teach hope skills using the Five Keys to Shine Hope. **You can remember the Five Keys with the mnemonic SHINE:**

S TRESS SKILLS	H APPINESS HABITS	I NSPIRED ACTIONS	N OURISHING NETWORKS	E LIMINATING CHALLENGES
90 second pause	Activating purpose	WOOP process	5:1 Rule	Limiting beliefs
Belly breathing	Pursuing passion	SMART goals	Compassion	Automatic Negative Thoughts (ANTs)
Journaling	Utilizing strengths	Stretch goals	Forgiveness	All-or-nothing thinking
Gardening	Meditation	Achievement goals	Love	Negative bias
Calming music	Smiling	Intrinsic goals	Gratitude	Rumination & Worry
Affirming beliefs	Exercising / Nutrition	Mastery goals	Recognition	Focusing on Uncontrollables
Sensory engagement	Creating / listening to music	Micro goals / Stepping	Support	Attaching to outcomes
Cold plunge	Dancing / Singing	Habit Stacking	Faith	Internalizing failure
Decluttering	Drawing / Painting	Visualization	Trust	Toxic Consumption
Prayer	Gratitude	Overcoming obstacles	Respect	Nocebo Effect
Nature walk	Volunteering	Regoaling	Effective Listening	Mind Wandering
Napping	Wonder / Awe	Write down goals / check in	Empathy	Implicity Bias
Laughter	Quality sleep		Kindness	Negative Framing
Crying	Doodling		Animals	Perfectionism Taking things personally
Tapping				
Yoga				
Mantras				

As you go through this guide, we will discuss each of the Five Keys to Shine Hope.

7 WAYS TO SHINE HOPE AS A FAMILY

Display Shine Posters Throughout the House

Use the 90-Second Pause

Practice Happiness Habits Together

Write Hope Hero Stories

Write My Shine Hope Stories

Create Family Goals, and Check Progress

Plant Sunflower Gardens for Hope (and practice Shine in the process)

7 Ways to Shine Hope As a Family

DISPLAY SHINE POSTERS THROUGHOUT THE HOUSE

Displaying Shine Hope posters around the home is a simple yet powerful way to help families stay connected with the practice of Shine Hope skills. These vibrant and engaging posters serve as daily reminders of the five key components—Stress Skills, Happiness Habits, Inspired Actions, Nourishing Networks, and Eliminating Challenges—that are essential for cultivating hope and well-being. By placing these visual cues in common areas, families can more easily integrate the Shine Hope skills into their everyday routines, creating a shared language and experience of hope.

When a family member is struggling or feeling overwhelmed, often referred to as being in their "downstairs brain" (the part of the brain associated with emotions, impulsive reactions, and survival instincts), the posters provide quick, accessible strategies to help them regain calm and clarity. Having these resources at hand is especially useful during moments of stress, as it can be challenging to recall coping techniques in the heat of the moment. The posters act as a roadmap, guiding family members back to a state of hope and regulation.

USE THE 90-SECOND PAUSE

When we are triggered by things in our environment, our fight or flight response is activated. And we have a flooding of stress chemicals that put us in our 'downstairs' brain, where we make very bad decisions. It takes a full 90-seconds, from the last point of trigger, for those chemicals to cycle through.

Taking a 90-second pause is critical for allowing those chemicals to cycle out, so we can get back 'upstairs', where we problem-solve, are kind, creative, and collaborative. Practice noticing when you or family members are in their 'downstairs brain', and see how you can take a 90 second pause to allow the situation time to diffuse. 90-seconds is a long time in tense situations, yet it can go a long way to making healthier decisions for ourselves, and others.

PRACTICE HAPPINESS HABITS TOGETHER

Practicing happiness habits as a family is a transformative way to nurture and grow hope within the household. Incorporating happiness habits into daily routines doesn't have to be complicated. It can be as simple as sharing a few things you are grateful for around the dinner table, or spending quality time playing a favorite game.

These moments of connection help shift the focus from daily stressors to positive experiences, fostering an optimistic outlook and helping us stay in our "upstairs brain"—the part of the brain associated with logical thinking, emotional regulation, and problem-solving. When we practice happiness habits, we strengthen our ability to remain in this upstairs brain, even when faced with stress or challenges. As a bonus, create a non-negotiable Happiness Habit list that you decide to make part of your daily practice (i.e. good sleep, nutrition, exercise).

WRITE HOPE HERO STORIES

Writing about a Hope Hero as a family is a powerful exercise that can grow hope and reduce stigma around struggles and challenges. A template for writing about a Hope Hero is found on page 42.

A Hope Hero is someone who embodies strength, perseverance, and the ability to overcome obstacles using the Shine Hope skills—whether it's a famous figure, a community member, or even a family member. By identifying and exploring the qualities of a Hope Hero, families can openly discuss the nature of challenges and the ways hope can be cultivated in difficult times

This exercise empowers family members to see that they too can embody the qualities of their Hope Hero. By discussing and writing together, families learn that hope isn't just something for extraordinary people—it's a skill they can build within themselves. This shared activity strengthens family bonds, creates a positive narrative around overcoming difficulties, and provides strategies for how to respond to challenges with hope.

WRITE MY SHINE HOPE STORIES

One excellent way of teaching kids the Shine framework is using our template for My Shine Hope Story (see page 39). We've also included an example on page 40.

Start by writing your own "My Shine Hope Story" to share with your child. Think about a time when you faced a challenge and how you used the Shine Hope skills to navigate it. Use the template provided to outline your story, describing how you applied each of the Shine skills to overcome the difficulty.

Once you've written your story, share it with your child in a way they can understand. Explain that everyone experiences challenges and that talking about them is a normal part of life. Sharing your story will help them see that hope and problem-solving are key to getting through tough times.

Next, work with your child to write their own "My Shine Hope Story" using the same template. Guide them through the process, encouraging them to use Shine Hope skills to reflect on and tackle their challenges. Continue to write new stories together as challenges arise; this ongoing practice will help normalize these conversations and teach your child how to use hope to overcome obstacles.

While writing My Shine Hope Stories, ensure that everyone in the house has someone in their Nourishing Network that they can turn to during challenges.

CREATE FAMILY GOALS, AND CHECK PROGRESS

Creating family goals is a great way to bond as a family, and make sure we are moving things forward together. It can be a SMART goal, or a stretch goal, just make sure it is a achievement goal! Then go through the stepping process, and chunk down all the things everyone needs to do to get there.

Accomplishing goals are one of the Happiness Habits, and achieving them together can create closer bonds. Make sure when you create the goal, you write them down, and check in with each other regularly to ensure progress. As you are up to 95% more likely to achieve it if you do so!

Want to do something extra as a family to really practice the skills? Volunteer and teach Hopeful Minds to kids in the Community or plant sunflower Gardens for Hope. Don't forget, hope is a journey, and a muscle you have to build. Keep Shining!

PLANT SUNFLOWER GARDENS FOR HOPE

Planting sunflowers, the international symbol for hope, are a great way to practice Shine Hope Skills. Consider planting a garden in your front yard, at your community, place of worship, or school. And then post one of our signs so that people can see hope is measurable, teachable, and get access to resources that helps them practice.

WHY SUNFLOWERS?

We were very deliberate in our choosing of the sunflowers. It all began from a study by the Emotional Impact of Flowers Study conducted by Jeannette M. Haviland-Jones, Ph.D., Professor of Psychology, Project Director, Human Development Lab at Rutgers. According to her research, regardless of age, flowers have an immediate impact on happiness. Recent studies have suggested flowers help reduce stress, and often increase serotonin and dopamine. As we further researched, we found:

- The symbolism of the sunflower holds profound meaning. A sunflower seed begins its journey in darkness, mirroring our most hopeless states. It represents our potential for growth and improvement amid despair. Just as a seed cannot flourish alone, we, too, rely on our Hope Network to nurture our hope.
- The growth of a sunflower echoes our journey toward hope. It stretches roots deep into the ground, akin to our efforts to break free from despair using Stress Skills—meditation, deep breathing, and mindful pauses.
- As the sunflower emerges into the sunlight, it unfurls leaves to gather sunshine, needing water, nourishment, and care to flourish. Similarly, we cultivate positive feelings through Happiness Habits—long-term, healthy practices fostering more and more hope.
- Obstacles pepper the sunflower's path; rocky soil and inadequate resources. Likewise, we face challenges. However, equipped with Stress Skills, Happiness Habits, Inspired Actions, Nourishing Networks, and skills to Eliminate Challenges, we navigate and conquer these hurdles.
- The sunflower's purpose transcends its growth; it provides sustenance and joy. Similarly, we share hope with those around us, becoming beacons of optimism and joy.
- Our choice of the sunflower and its vibrant yellow hue isn't arbitrary. It symbolizes our commitment to shine a positive light on hope, eradicating mental health stigma through proactive measures in prevention, research, and education. Yellow is the color of happiness and hope.
- Gardening is also very healthy for the mood, so we encourage community gardens. Eating sunflower seeds can be healthy for the brain, as they are rich in vital nutrients. It is also one of the only flowers that can be planted anywhere in the world, and we believe the 'how' to hope must be planted everywhere as well.
- It is also a method for nonprofits to raise funds for hope. You can sell the seeds, have gardens sponsored, sell products in retail, or create art for auctions. The ideas are endless!

So, in this endeavor, the sunflower becomes more than a symbol—it becomes the embodiment of hope, illuminating pathways toward a brighter future for cities and individuals alike.

PLANT SUNFLOWER GARDENS TO SHINE HOPE

Gardening is a great time to practice the Shine Hope Framework, as we have a lot of challenges while planting a garden and we can go from hope to hopelessness pretty quickly. Yet that is a normal part of life, so gardening is an easy place to start practicing these skills.

Say you find some tough ground you need to dig into to plant, you may get frustrated and give up. It is a good time to practice a **Stress Skill** like a 90-second pause or deep breathing, to calm down your stress response. Then try again! You may also notice when others get frustrated and teach them how to use this skill to navigate from their downstairs brain back upstairs.

Eating the sunflower seeds (if ok with your doctor) might be a good way for you to practice your **Happiness Habits.** Sunflower seeds are nutritious, high in choline and selenium, great for brain function and memory. You might also get some exercise planting gardens, and spend time in nature, two other Happiness Habits and great ways to release endorphins.

Planting gardens remind us to take **Inspired Actions** by setting specific goals for the garden. If we want a garden, we need to set a SMART goal about how many flowers, when and where we want the garden, and how we are going to grow the flowers. It is best if we write down the plan, chunk it down into actionable steps, think about obstacles and multiple ways we might overcome them, and check in with someone regularly to ensure progress.

We can cultivate our **Nourishing Networks** by planting gardens with others. That way, if we have challenges while planting, we can face them together and be more creative about overcoming them. And if we don't live by the person we want to plant with, we can both decide to plant and check in regularly on the garden. It is also super fun to plan community gardens, or even fields of sunflowers, and all join together in learning and practicing skills to Shine Hope.

And finally, time to get serious about **Eliminating Challenges**. For example, if our sunflowers die and we fail for a season of planting, it is easy for us to think of ourselves as failures. Yet we aren't failures, our process failed. So deconstruct the process. Did we under or over water? Did we plant at the wrong time of year? Was something wrong with the soil? Did we overwater? It is time to investigate, and instead of ruminating about the sunflowers start figuring out what we can do better to try again next year.

Planting sunflowers is a way to spread the message of hope, as if you put up a Gardens of Hope sign with the website, people can then find the curriculum to learn more about the programs for 'how' to hope. Our program is available around the world, and gardens are a great way to share the message that Hope is Teachable.

Find out more at www.hopefulcities.org   @theshinehopecompany

HOW TO PLANT SUNFLOWERS AT HOME

To plant your sunflowers from seeds:

- Sunflowers should be planted between May and July (depending on where you live, you will need to look at your specific climate) once the last frost has melted.

- Space seeds 12 to 48 inches apart, depending on the size of your sunflower variety.

- Seeds should be placed 1 to 2 inches deep in clayey soils and 2+ inches deep in sandy soils.

- A small amount of fertilizer mixed in during planting will encourage root growth.

- While the sunflowers are growing, water around the root zone (3 to 4 inches from the plant) once a day.

- Once the plants are established, water less frequently but more deeply.

Most sunflower varieties will mature in 80 to 120 days. Once sunflowers develop seeds, harvest seeds with students to save for planting next season. As you can see, lots of fun ways to practice how to Shine Hope when we garden. Share with us how it went for you, pictures from your sunflowers, ways you practiced your skills, and help us all get better.

Tag us @theshinehopecompany @ifredorg #ShineHope #GardensForHope #Hope

STRESS SKILLS

Stress Skills are actions that help you navigate your stress response and work through your body's chemical response to external stimuli. By practicing them, you are teaching yourself how to proactively manage the emotional despair found in hopelessness and move towards positive feelings where you activate hope.

The Stress Response

This is when you are emotionally triggered by something in your environment, and you go into fight, flight, freeze, or fawn mode as your body releases stress hormones, such as cortisol, adrenaline, and norepinephrine. You are in your downstairs brain, and can't reach your upstairs brain; the upstairs brain is the place where you make good decisions for moving towards all you hope for in life.

90 second pause	Sensory engagement	Laughter
Belly breathing	Cold plunge	Crying
Journaling	Decluttering	Tapping
Gardening	Prayer	Yoga
Calming music	Nature walk	Mantras
Affirming beliefs	Napping	

© The Shine Hope Company, LLC

Stress Skills

Stress Skills are the First Key to Shine Hope. When you are emotionally triggered by something in your environment, your body has a physiological response. By practicing Stress Skills, you are teaching yourself how to work through your body's chemical response to external stimuli and gain control of your emotions before you react. Stress Skills include breathing techniques, meditation, music, nature, and journaling, but find what works for you when you feel stressed or triggered. These are just some examples of Stress Skills, yet you might find others that work better for you. Test them all out. You will find that, by using Stress Skills, your children calm themselves down more quickly during times of stress (as will you!). By teaching your children Stress Skills, you will be teaching them how to work through their body's chemical response to external stimuli and then respond calmly.

ALLOSTATIC LOAD

We all experience stress, it's entirely normal. **Experts** believe we need a certain amount of stress to function at an optimum level because stress motivates us to make changes and reach our goals.

However, persistent stress leads to many negative consequences that can have a lasting effect on our overall health and well-being; this is called the allostatic load. We experience the allostatic load when the challenges we face in our environment exceed our ability to cope.

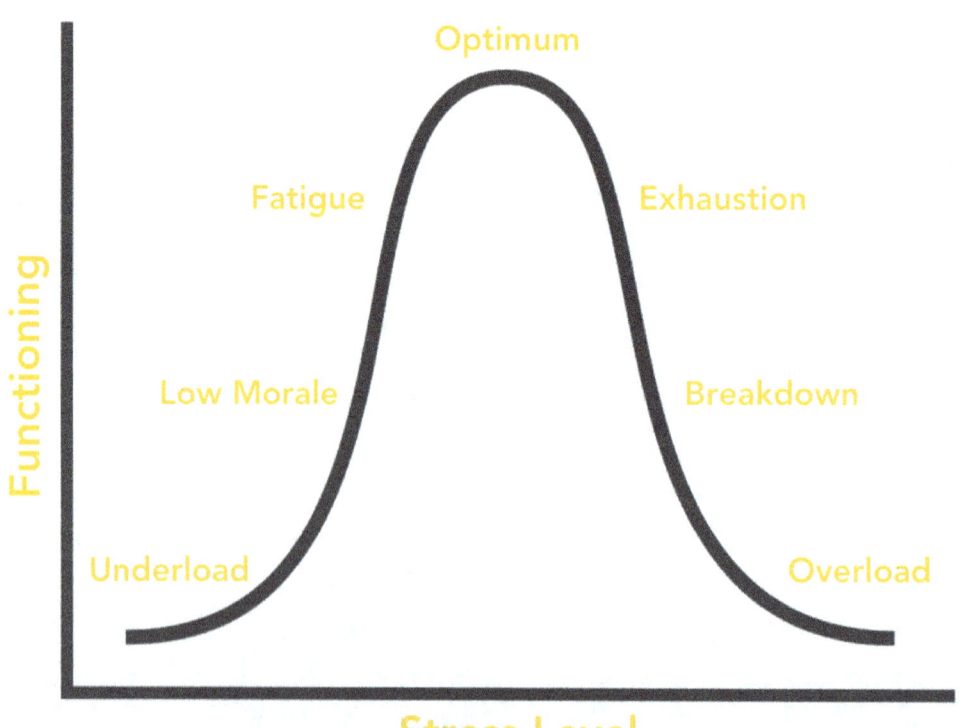

POSITIVE FEELINGS AND INSPIRED ACTIONS

Hope is fueled by two main ingredients: positive feelings and inspired actions. When kids experience negative feelings, we want to teach them not to dismiss them. Instead, we should encourage children to experience all of their feelings, learn how to express their negative ones in healthy ways, and then get themselves back to positive feelings before taking any action.

WHAT ARE FEELINGS?

Feelings are responses to specific events in your environment. You can first identify an emotion or feeling through physical changes in your body, such as a racing heart, flushed cheeks, or a tightened jaw.

We can react to an event through our upstairs brain or our downstairs brain. The key is to learn how to identify and observe feelings in order to respond through our upstairs, more rational brain.

This is a crucial concept to teach children; they must understand that emotions are not inherently good or bad; it is how you choose to react to the emotion that can be good or bad.

POSITIVE FEELINGS VS. NEGATIVE FEELINGS

Positive feelings are those feelings that help us to stay hopeful as we work towards our goals. Feelings are not good or bad; they just are. Yet if we act immediately when we are in negative feeling states, we increase our likelihood of negative actions. In order to foster positive feelings, we must go through the following process:

- Identify the emotion we are feeling.
- Determine if it is a positive feeling that will help us achieve our goals.
- If it is a negative feeling, release the energy associated with the feeling using Stress Skills *(download the Hopeful Minds Overview Curriculum to learn more about stress skills you can use)*.
- Use Happiness Habits to focus our energy once again on fostering positive feelings and cultivating Hope.

This was reproduced with the permission of Friendship Bench. See all their amazing work, and learn how to bring a friendship bench to your community, at www.friendshipbenchzimbabwe.org

STRESS SKILLS INCLUDE:

90 second pause	Sensory engagement	Laughter
Belly breathing	Cold plunge	Crying
Journaling	Decluttering	Tapping
Gardening	Prayer	Yoga
Calming music	Nature walk	Mantras
Affirming beliefs	Napping	

You will find that, by using Stress Skills, your children will be able to more quickly calm themselves down during times of stress. Once they have calmed down and released the energy associated with their negative emotions, they will then be able to respond calmly with their upstairs brain.

HOW TO TEACH STRESS SKILLS AT HOME

Teaching Stress Skills in your home is easy! When your children are upset, try the following:

- **90-second rule:** Create a 90-second rule in your home. When they come to you upset, encourage them to breathe deeply with their eyes closed for 90 seconds before they talk to you. You can learn more about deep breathing exercises in our Hopeful Minds Overview: 3 Lesson Curriculum.

- **Grounding:** When your child is in stressful situations outside of the home, encourage them to tell you what they notice with each of their five senses. Focusing on the present moment with our five senses can help us break our stress and worry cycles.

- **Visualize:** Encourage your children to take time to visualize the night before big tests, games, and performances. Visualizing success the night before can help decrease stress during the real event.

- **Stress Skills:** When you notice your child becoming stressed, pull out the list of Stress Skills and work with them to pick one and practice it together.

HAPPINESS HABITS

Happiness Habits are healthy, long-term actions that cause your brain to release happiness hormones including endorphins, dopamine, serotonin, and oxytocin. Happiness Habits help you stay in your upstairs brain, where you access the problem-solving skills, collaboration, and passion critical for hope.

Positive Feelings

Positive feelings, the first ingredient of hope, are feelings that are located in your upstairs brain like wonder, joy, and peace that make it easier to overcome obstacles that get in the way of hope. You proactively manage the emotional despair of hopelessness using Stress Skills and use your Happiness Habits to stay in your upstairs brain, where you then energetically move towards your goals in life.

Activating purpose	Exercising / Nutrition	Volunteering
Pursuing passion	Creating / listening to music	Wonder / Awe
Utilizing strengths	Dancing / Singing	Quality sleep
Meditation	Drawing / Painting	Doodling
Smiling	Gratitude	

© The Shine Hope Company, LLC

Happiness Habits

Happiness Habits are the Second Key to Shine Hope. They are healthy, long-term actions that you can take to foster positive feelings and stay hopeful. In general, positive feelings are typically linked to happiness. Happiness comes in the form of self-confidence, good sleep, increased memory retention, relief of anxiety and depression, and energy towards goal achievement. Simple things like physical activity can create positive feelings for our children – a key ingredient to hope.

HAPPINESS HABITS INCLUDE:

Activating purpose	Exercising / Nutrition	Volunteering
Pursuing passion	Creating / listening to music	Wonder / Awe
Utilizing strengths	Dancing / Singing	Quality sleep
Meditation	Drawing / Painting	Doodling
Smiling	Gratitude	

HOW TO TEACH HAPPINESS HABITS AT HOME

Consider the following ideas:

- **S.M.A.R.T Goals:** Set S.M.A.R.T. goals together and have weekly family check-ins to see how everyone's goals are progressing (see below for more information).

- **Gratitude:** Every night, have your children list one thing they were thankful for today and one act of kindness they saw today. Ending your day with a focus on positivity is a great way to stimulate a positive attitude for the upcoming day.

- **Nutrition:** Fruits and veggies are not only good for your body; they are also good for your brain! Making sure kids get hope-helping fruits and vegetables every day can help them stay hopeful, happy, and healthy.

- **Happiness Habits:** Have your child review the Happiness Habits we've listed and encourage them to practice one a day for a week.

INSPIRED ACTIONS

Inspired Actions, the second ingredient of hope, are the deliberate steps you take toward your goals in life. Inspired Actions help you to move away from the motivational helplessness, the second ingredient of hopelessness, and toward what you are hopeful for in life.

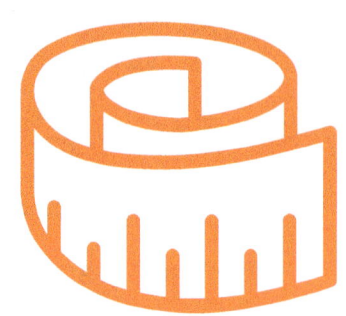

Types of Goals:

WOOP	SMART
Achievement	Stretch
Intrinsic	Micro-Goals

Pathways, Agency, and Regoaling

Obstacles are inevitable, and sometimes you can't reach the goal as you intended. It is important to embrace obstacles to goals, learn to pivot or reevaluate, be flexible and adaptable, and never be afraid to ask for help.

If a goal seems too big, use the stepping process or create micro-goals to chunk it down into smaller goals. Think of one thing you can do in the next 20 minutes. And know when you need to re-goal.

© The Shine Hope Company, LLC

Inspired Actions

The Third Key to Shine Hope is **Inspired Actions.** Goals help you maintain hope by giving you something to look forward to and encouraging you to work towards your future. Using inspired actions to pursue your purpose and reach your goals can help you maintain hope.

WOOP

One way to establish your goals is by using the WOOP method. The WOOP method includes four steps, each of which is outlined below: **W(wish), O(outcome), O(obstacle), and P(plan):**

WISH
Think about your purpose. What is the most important wish or concern related to your purpose? Pick a wish that is challenging but that you can still fulfill.

OUTCOME
What would be the best possible outcome if your wish came true? How would fulfilling your wish make you feel?

OBSTACLE
What is within you or in your environment that keeps you from fulfilling your wish?

PLAN
Identify one action you can take or thought you can think to overcome your obstacle. Then, make an if-then plan: IF (I encounter this obstacle) THEN (I will use this solution).

SMART GOALS

"SMART"-goal-setting is an evidence-based approach that is used universally at any scale – from individual goals to big business strategies. We want to strengthen our hope muscles through positive feelings and, in turn, this inspired SMART action.

SMART goals should be:

SPECIFIC
Be specific and think about these questions when creating your goal: Who and what do you need? What do you want to achieve? How much time is needed? Where is this happening? Why is this goal important to you?

MEASURABLE
Can you measure your progress? If this goal will take a long time to achieve, set shorter term goals to reach along the way.

ACHIEVABLE
Are you inspired and motivated to reach your goal? Do you have the tools or skills you need? If not, do you know how you can get them?

RELEVANT
Does your goal make sense? Does it go along with what you are trying to achieve in the bigger picture?

TIME-BOUND
Is your timing realistic? Can you achieve your goal in the time period set? Think about what you may want to achieve at the halfway point.

HOW TO TEACH INSPIRED ACTIONS AT HOME

Family Goal-Setting: We recommend not only setting SMART goals for yourself but also helping your children set their own SMART goals. Working on individual goals as a family can help inspire positive feelings and enthusiasm, both of which are required to reach our goals.

GOAL WORKSHEET

Use this worksheet regularly in your goal setting process. Feel free to copy and complete for multiple goals, including family, relationships, health, and community. And remember to set some stretch goals, which takes you beyond the SMART process.

MY GOAL: _____

IS IT:

○ **S**PECIFIC ○ **M**EASURABLE ○ **A**CHIEVABLE ○ **R**ELEVANT ○ **T**IME-BOUND

○ NO, IT'S A STRETCH GOAL! :)

Is your goal an achievement goal? ○ YES ○ NO

Is your goal an intrinsic goal? ○ YES ○ NO

What are the feelings associated with achieving this goal?	Why do you want to achieve this goal?	What positive affirmation am I willing to say daily to achieve this goal?

To support this goal, I commit to regular practice of:

Three Stress Skills	Three Happiness Habits	Eliminating These Challenges
1.	1.	1.
2.	2.	2.
3.	3.	3.

What are six steps or microgoals that will help me reach my goal?

1. _____ 4. _____

2. _____ 5. _____

3. _____ 6. _____

Name 3 obstacles towards my goals:

1.
2.
3.

Name multiple ways to overcome each:

Name one person I can check in with regularly on this goal:

What step can I take in the next five minutes to get closer to my goal.

Contact this person now and make a regular appointment to check in.

○ Done.

Learn How to Shine Hope™, and Build Hopeful Mindsets® at:

the shine hope company

NOURISHING NETWORKS

Your Nourishing Networks, also known as your Hope Networks, are the people in your life that provide you with support, help you stay on track, encourage you to succeed, and who you do the same for in return. You are up to 95% more likely to achieve a goal if you write it down, and check in with someone regularly. So Nourishing Networks are critical support systems for moving you towards what you hope for in life.

Your Hope Networks should include:

- People who know and understand you.
- People who value your strengths.
- People who activate the SHINE framework.
- People whom you trust and can confide in.
- People who are available to support you.
- People you are willing to do the above for as well.

Enhancing Your Hope Networks

Enhance your Hope Networks using the 5:1 rule, vulnerability, praise, recognition, kindness, gratitude, empathy, compassion, collaboration, and strong communication, and be sure to have different networks for different areas of life.

Don't forget to include doctors, therapists, and/or other medical professionals in your Hope Networks.

© The Shine Hope Company, LLC

Nourishing Networks

The Fourth Key to Shine Hope is **Nourishing Networks.** Your Nourishing Network, or Hope Network, is the group of people around you who know you, appreciate you, see your strengths, and help you keep your hopeful attitude. People in your Hope Network can help your hope fight hopelessness, stress, and anxiety.

HOW TO TEACH NOURISHING NETWORKS AT HOME

You may find, when thinking about a Hope Network, that your child struggles to identify someone who is in their Hope Network. It is important to remember that you, as a parent or guardian, can be one of those supports for your children. It is also important to remind your children that Hope Networks are not fixed; they will continue to grow and change each and every day. As you make your way through the school year, encourage your children to continue reaching out and building a strong Hope Network. You can help them strengthen their Hope Network using kindness, empathy, praise, recognition, and strong communication.

Identify faculty/staff within your childrens' school, such as the school nurse, social worker, teacher, or counselor, that your children can reach out to in times of need. Remember, hope is both behavioral and biological, so if a child is having challenges with hope, it is important to also help get them to proper medical care, when needed.

By understanding the impact of hopelessness, we reinforce and highlight the importance of building hope with our young generations.

It is also important to help your child understand the importance of health versus unhealthy relationships by recognizing the signs of unhealthy relationships. Check out this article on Psych Central on the signs of toxic relationships (https://psychcentral.com/relationships/signs-of-toxic-relationships). It is true with friends, too. Look at this article in Psychology Today about 8 signs of a toxic friendship.

Lastly, your teen may have difficulties navigating a break up, whether it's with a friend or a significant other. Breakups disrupt routines and challenge the preference for consistency, making it a challenging experience. Breakups can also bring up hopelessness and subsequent anxiety and depression. Help your teen manage breakups by reminding them to use Stress Skills while feeling the emotions that arise from the break up. Allow them to talk through their thoughts about the breakup, and help them find closure.

NOURISHING NETWORK

Directions: Write or draw answers to each of the prompts below.

Friends and family I can count on and confide in:

People I turn to for Stress Skills:

People I practice Happiness Habits with:

Things I can connect to:
ex. Spiritual Advisor, Peer Support, Animals, Nature, etc.

Teachers, doctors, and experts I go to for support:

Community Resources I can utilize:

Where can I go to in times of crisis? ex. If you can't list anyone, you can check out our list of resources for how to get connected. Visit https://hopefulcities.org/get-support/

One person I can always count on even if we aren't close:

Challenges to Hope are negative habits of thought that quickly take you to hopelessness, that emotional despair and sense of helplessness. The thought patterns are often unconscious habits, so becoming aware of these patterns is critical. Once we know what they are and recognize them, it is important to counteract them so that we don't let them keep us from all we hope for in life.

Eliminating Challenges

Most of the Challenges to Hope take constant, repetitive actions to change and overcome. Thanks to the science of neuroplasticity, we know it is possible with practice and dedication. The key is to learn to identify what specific challenges happen most frequently and then proactively find ways to manage those challenges.

- Limiting beliefs
- Automatic Negative Thoughts (ANTs)
- All-or-nothing thinking
- Negative bias
- Rumination & Worry
- Focusing on Uncontrollables
- Attaching to outcomes
- Internalizing failure
- Toxic Consumption
- Nocebo Effect
- Mind Wandering
- Implicity Bias
- Negative Framing
- Perfectionism Taking things personally

© The Shine Hope Company, LLC

Eliminating Challenges

The Fifth Key to Shine Hope is **Eliminating Challenges.** As discussed at the beginning of this guide, challenges to hope are things that move us from hope to hopelessness. By teaching children the Five Keys to Shine Hope, we are arming them with the skills they need to eliminate challenges to hope.

Some of the most common challenges to hope include:

Limiting Beliefs: Limiting beliefs are the negative beliefs that you have about yourself and your abilities. It is important to challenge your children to identify their limiting beliefs and replace them with reaffirming beliefs.

ANTs (Automatic Negative Thoughts): These are subconscious, repetitive, negative thoughts that you have about yourself, your surroundings, or specific situations. Like limiting beliefs, it's important to encourage your children to replace ANTs with positive thoughts.

All-or-Nothing Thinking: This is when you only think in extremes rather than in shades of gray. Rather than seeing all of the solutions to a problem, all-or-nothing thinking forces you to see either complete success or complete failure. When you start to hear your children use absolute terms like "never" or "always," it's important to encourage them to take deep breaths and reframe those thoughts.

Negative Bias: Negative bias refers to the psychological phenomenon that causes negative events to have a greater impact on our brains than positive ones. We tend to fixate on a criticism rather than a compliment, pay more attention to bad news than good news, and notice negative events happening near us instead of positive ones. Negative bias forces us into our downstairs brain, and can have lasting impacts on our relationships, behavior, and hope.

Rumination: Rumination refers to repeatedly going over a thought or a problem from your past, without end. Rumination is associated with numerous negative mental states, including depression and post-traumatic stress disorder. Help your children learn to identify their rumination cycles and then use Stress Skills, such as engaging their senses, to get back to the present moment.

Worry: Worry is when you feel anxious or afraid about real or imagined future scenarios. Where rumination focuses on the past, worry focuses on the future. Worry forces you to fixate on and respond to the future dangers that you think you may encounter. Like ruminating, worrying can be detrimental to your mental and physical health. They say about 85% of what we worry about never happens. When your children find themselves worrying, help them engage their senses and return to the present moment, then use Happiness Habits to stay in the present moment.

Focusing on Uncontrollables: When you focus on trying to control things that are out of your control, it leads to helplessness and despair, the two ingredients of hopelessness. Whenever your children encounter new obstacles, take time to discuss what they can control and what they cannot control. Then, help them use Stress Skills to release the feelings associated with the things they can't control.

Attaching to Outcomes: Attaching to outcomes is when we set goals, and are then unable or willing to be satisfied unless we reach that specific goal. While goal setting is important, it is also important to have a sense of active surrender and know that sometimes there is a better path. Being too attached to specific goal attainment leads to hopelessness when we don't reach that goal.

Internalizing Failure: Internalizing failure is when you fail at something (e.g., a test, game, relationship, etc.) and then believe that it means that you are a failure. We lose many children to suicide each year because they fail a test or a relationship, and then decide that it means that they are failures. Yet when you fail, it means that a step in your process failed; it does not mean that you are a failure. It is incredibly important to continually reframe your children's relationship with failure and help them see that failure means they are growing and improving. When they fail at something, help them deconstruct the process and figure out what went wrong and what they can do differently next time.

By using the Five Keys to Shine Hope and implementing hope language in your home, you can ensure that no matter what challenges your children face, they will always find their way from hopelessness to hope.

HOW TO TEACH ELIMINATING CHALLENGES AT HOME

- **Encourage Positive Self-Talk:** Teach your child to use positive language when faced with a challenge. Help them replace self-doubt with affirmations like, "I can handle this" or "I will find a way through." Eliminating negative thoughts is a crucial part of managing challenges and fostering a hopeful mindset.

- **Create a Safe Space for Open Communication:** Encourage your child to share their feelings, worries, and challenges without fear of judgment. Listen actively and show empathy, helping them understand that everyone faces difficulties. When children feel safe discussing their struggles, they're better equipped to address and eliminate them.

MY SHINE HOPE STORY™

HOW HOPEFUL ARE YOU?
Did you measure your hope? The lower your score, the more you want to practice these skills! Remember, hope is a muscle we need to build it (add it).

Check out here to get your hope score.

To write your own shine hope story, spend 20% of your time writing about your challenge, and 80% of the time sharing strategies for how you overcame it so others can learn from you. Here's how:

1. Write your name in the yellow line next to the box (feel free to use a nickname or anything else).

2. Put your favorite photo on the yellow box, or an image of something that represents you.

3. Write an introduction to your story explaining the challenge you faced. Explain the two ingredients of hopelessness: despair (feelings) and helplessness (inability to act) you experienced.

 4. Share sadness, anger, fear, or other feelings, and choose **3 Stress Skills** you used to naviate them (from the Shine infographic, or choose your own!).

 5. Share **3 Happiness Habits** you used to get back to your upstairs brain.

 6. Talk about **3 Inspired Actions** you took, or share how you chunked down goals, the types of goals you set, or if you had to regoal.

 7. Share who was in your **Nourishing Network**, and how they helped you navigate the challenge.

 8. Pick 3 challenges from the **'Eliminating Challenges'** on the infographic, and share how you eliminated them.

 9. Write your conclusion. What do you want the world to know? What do you wish someone had told you? What is the moral of the story?

If you're inspired, share your story so we can help activate these skills globally.

#Hope #ShineHope #MyShineHopeStory

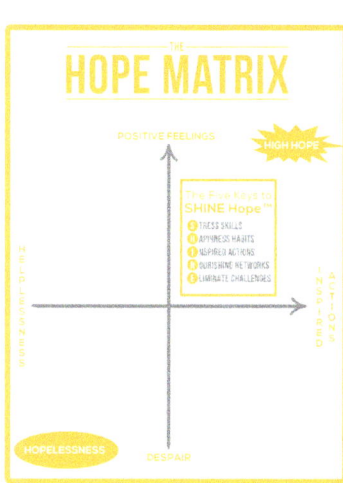

> We all experience moments of hopelessness (emotional despair and motivational helplessness). The key is to use the Shine Hope skills to navigate your way from despair to positive feelings, and helplessness to inspired actions. Use the Shine Hope framework to build your muscle.

© 2024 The Shine Hope Company LLC.

MY SHINE HOPE STORY™

☀ Kathryn Goetzke

When I was 18 years old, a freshman at the University of Iowa, I called home and heard an unfamiliar, deep voice on the other line. It wasn't anyone I recognized, and he asked for my mom. My mom got on the phone to tell me my dad had taken his life. In that instance, my whole world crumbled. I felt a sadness so deep I thought I would never survive, and a helplessness so profound as I could not bring him back.

As hard as it was, I had to move forward. I started using Stress Skills to manage my pain. I cried when I was sad, started boxing to manage my anger, and learned how to start belly breathing to manage my fear. I listened to a lot of calming music when things got hard, and I started hiking all over the world. I also learned how to use sensory engagement to bring myself to the present moment.

Happiness Habits were critical. Sleep became an important part of my routine, and I started eating healthier foods. I cut alcohol out of my life. I replaced smoking with running, and made comedy clubs and laughter a part of my life. I listened to music, turned my sensory engagement passion into a purpose and started a company, and made volunteering a regular part of my life. I used dancing and live concerts (like my fave The Killers) as a form of release.

I also was very intentional about Inspired Actions. I had to chunk down my goals, leaving school and taking only one year at a time until I graduated. I had to regoal from having experiences with my dad to finding father-like figures to be in my life. I got closer to my brothers, their kids, and found mentors like Paul Carter and Dr. Belfer to guide me on my journey. My mom is my rock, my greatest source of strength and inspiration, keeping me moving forward towards my dreams.

Nourishing Networks were a constant. I stayed close to my friends and family, traveling, dancing, studying, and laughing. They were so compassionate, kind, generous, fun, and helped me heal. I forgave my dad for leaving, and forgave myself for not being there for him when he needed me. I got very close to God, understanding that I couldn't save my dad, and that in time this lesson would teach me how to help others.

It wasn't easy to Eliminate Challenges like rumination, internalizing failure, or worry. Yet I studied sensory engagement to be present when my mind started running. I deconstructed what led to my dad taking his life in a way that made it clear how to save myself and others. I knew that I couldn't control my dad, just like I can't control others. So I have focused on creating programming yet not being attached to if people want to learn it.

It's not been the easiest journey, and takes work. Yet by using the Shine Hope framework I have created a new life that is full of wonder, awe, happiness, adventure, and meaning. A different one than I expected, yet a beautiful one because I was able to dive in my pain, and learn the lessons necessary to teach others. And I use all my dad taught me in business to create a Shine Hope model for the world that ensures all know the what, why, and how of hope. And for that I know he is so very proud.

No matter what life brings, Keep Shining.

#Hope #ShineHope #MyHopeStory

© 2024 The Shine Hope Company LLC.

MY SHINE HOPE STORY™

#Hope #ShineHope #MyHopeStory
© 2024 The Shine Hope Company LLC.

MY HOPE HERO

HOW HOPEFUL ARE YOU?
Did you measure your hope? The lower your score, the more you want to practice these skills! Remember, hope is a muscle we need to build it (add it).

Check out here to get your hope score.

To write your hope hero journey, spend 20% of your time writing about their challenge, and 80% of the time sharing strategies for how they overcame it so others can learn from it. Here's how:

 1. Write your hope hero's name in the yellow line next to the box (feel free to use a nickname or anything else).

 2. Put your favorite photo of them on the yellow box, or an image of something that represents your hope hero.

 3. Write an introduction explaining the challenge they faced. Explain the two ingredients of hopelessness: despair (feelings) and helplessness (inability to act) they experienced.

 4. Share sadness, anger, fear, or other feelings, and choose 3 **Stress Skills** they used to navigate them (from the Shine infographic, or choose your own!).

 5. Share 3 **Happiness Habits** they used to get back to upstairs brain.

 6. Talk about 3 **Inspired Actions** they took, or share how your hope hero chunked down goals, the types of goals they've set, or if they had to regoal.

 7. Share who was in their **Nourishing Network**, and how it helped them navigate the challenge.

 8. Pick 3 challenges from the **'Eliminating Challenges'** on the infographic, and share how your hope hero eliminated them.

 9. Write the conclusion. What do you want the world to know? What do you wish someone had told you? What is the moral of the story?

If you're inspired, share this hope hero story so we can help activate these skills globally!

#Hope #ShineHope #MyHopeHero

> We all experience moments of hopelessness (emotional despair and motivational helplessness). The key is to use the Shine Hope skills to navigate your way from despair to positive feelings, and helplessness to inspired actions. Use the Shine Hope framework to build your muscle.

© 2024 The Shine Hope Company LLC.

MY HOPE HERO

#Hope #ShineHope #MyHopeStory

Resources for Stress, Anxiety, and Depression

CHILDREN AND STRESS

Stress is the product of the demands that are placed on us, and a normal part of life. It is not stress that kills us, it is our inability to effectively manage stress. Friends, family, jobs, or school can create stress, as well as a disconnection between what we think we should be accomplishing and what we are actually able to accomplish.

Children are not immune to stress, and if your child is feeling stress they are not alone. Some research suggests children are even more stressed than adults in these times. There are many reasons your children may encounter stress. Our Hopeful Minds program addresses stress, and provides stress management techniques, including the key 90 second rule. Our goal is to share additional insights, and provide tips on what else you might do at home.

As children grow, academic and social pressures, world news, and external trauma can become stressors at an increasing rate. The symptoms of stress can vary; however, the following list contains some of the more common symptoms typically identified in children suffering from stress:

- Stomachaches, Headaches and Nightmares
- Trouble concentrating or completing schoolwork
- Overreacting to minor problems
- Becoming clingy
- Becoming withdrawn or spending more time alone
- Short-term behavioral changes, such as mood swings, acting out, bedwetting, and changes in sleep pattern
- Younger children may start thumb sucking, hair twirling, and nose picking
- Older children may begin lying, bullying, or defying authority
- Drastic changes in academic performance

SOLUTIONS TO STRESS

There are healthy ways to help children both cope with and minimize stressors in their lives. We've provided a number of solutions in our Hopeful Minds program, and encourage you to do it with them so they start to recognize "stress," know how it feels in their body, and proactively manage it. It isn't stress that hurts us, it is our inability to manage stress. In addition to practicing hope strategies with them, you can support your child in managing their stress in the following ways:

AT HOME

- Make sure your child is getting proper rest and nutrition. Children need a well-balanced diet and 9-12 hours of sleep each night to stay physically and mentally healthy.
- Ensure your home is a physically and emotionally safe place for your child to come home to.
- Commit to a routine.
- Monitor the amount of screen time, as well as the television, video game, and book content your child is ingesting. The following two articles give excellent insights into the problems that can arise from too much screen time during childhood.
  - https://gabb.com/blog/how-smart-phones-affect-brain-development/
  - https://gabb.com/blog/austin-weirichs-story/
- Don't overschedule. Too many extracurricular activities can increase stress.
- Take time to talk through changes with your child before they happen.
- Encourage children to perform visualization and breathing activities prior to stressful events, such as games and tests.
- Learn to listen to problems without being critical or solving the problems for them. Help your children find their own solutions to situations that are adding stress to their lives.
- At the start of conversations with your children, establish whether they want you to listen, give advice, or take action based on the information they are sharing.
- Provide affection and encouragement.
- Adopt healthy habits, such as exercise and self-care, to manage your own stress in healthy ways. Children are perceptive and will pick up on how you react to your own stressors.

AT SCHOOL

- Involve students in social, club, and athletic activities where they can succeed.
- Use positive reinforcement and methods of discipline that promote self-esteem.
- Limit homework overload.
- Take time to actively listen to students and help them find ways to decrease stressors in their lives.
- Use frequent "movement" breaks between lessons to keep students active and engaged.
- Schedule time to organize. Especially in lower grades, providing time to organize desks and cubbies, sharpen pencils, and put away toys and tools can give students a greater sense of control.
- Establish a routine and implement your own time management techniques. A hectic classroom schedule is a common stressor for students.

- Encourage students to perform visualization and breathing activities prior to stressful events, such as games and tests.
- Pay attention to behavioral changes in your students. If concerning behaviors are continually exhibited, reach out to parents and/or a counselor.
- Provide patience and encouragement.

CHILDREN AND ANXIETY

When stress is not properly mitigated, it can lead to anxiety. Anxiety disorders negatively impact a child's life in many ways. Most children have fears and worries that appear at different times during development. Although fears and worries are normal, persistent or extreme fears may be due to anxiety.

The general rule is if any of these symptoms appear for two or more weeks, and are disrupting your child's daily life and activities, it is best to seek advice from a medical professional. The following is a list of symptoms that may help you determine if your child is experiencing anxiety:

- Distress during separation
- Phobias
- Fear and discomfort in social settings
- Excessive worry about the future and bad things happening
- Abnormal irritation or anger
- Trouble sleeping and fatigue
- Headaches and Stomachaches
- Repeated episodes of sudden, unexpected fear that come with symptoms such as heart pounding, trouble breathing, feeling dizzy, shaking, and sweating

MANAGING ANXIETY

As a parent or teacher, your goal isn't to eliminate a child's anxiety, but to help them learn to manage it. If you believe your child may have anxiety, it is important to take active steps to get your child the help they need including talking to a medical professional like your primary care doctor, or a therapist.

There is no shame in seeking support. Just as you would encourage your child to get support for heart or lung issues, kids need to feel comfortable seeking help for their brain. Mental health is a unique interplay of behavioral and biological exchange, so it is important to work on both. You can help them manage their anxiety in the following ways:

AT HOME

- Consult with your child's pediatrician or family physician. A mental health assessment and evaluation can be done for a diagnosis and treatment plan. Your doctor may refer you to a mental health professional such as a psychiatrist, psychologist, or counselor. *(Do not delay treatment. Early detection and diagnosis are important for getting your child the help they need. Though parents or guardians can often feel responsible for what is happening with their children, they did not cause the anxiety.)*
- Respect your child's feelings but don't empower the feelings. It is important to acknowledge that their feelings are real and valid and help them find the source of the anxiety they are feeling. However, once they have acknowledged their anxiety, it is important to help children learn to face their fears. Make sure you are not reinforcing fears with your behaviors.
- Make sure your child is getting proper rest and nutrition. Children need a well-balanced diet and 9-12 hours of sleep each night to stay physically and mentally healthy.
- Ensure your home is a physically and emotionally safe place for your child to come home to.
- Commit to a routine.
- Monitor the amount of screen time, as well as the television, video game, and book content your child is ingesting.
- Practice mindfulness and relaxation techniques.
- Take time to talk through changes with your child before they happen. Preparing for upcoming changes can help remove the anxiety associated with them.
- At the start of conversations with your children, establish whether they want you to listen, give advice, or take action based on the information they are sharing.
- Help your child with problem-solving skills. Develop a plan of realistic steps your child can take toward a goal, recognize their success on the path, and encourage the enjoyment of the experience along the way. Help identify potential obstacles or difficulties and plan/talk about ways to overcome them. Focus on strengths.
- Adopt healthy habits to manage your own anxieties. Children are perceptive and will pick up on how you react to your own anxieties.
- Have conversations with your children about failure. It is important for them to understand that everyone fails at things and that when they fail, it does not mean that they are failures.

AT SCHOOL

- Use positive reinforcement and methods of discipline that promote self-esteem.
- Respect your student's feelings but don't empower the feelings. It is important to acknowledge that their feelings are valid and help them find the source of the anxiety they are feeling. However, once they have acknowledged their anxiety, it is important to help children learn to face their fears. Make sure you are not reinforcing fears with your behaviors.
- Limit homework overload.
- Take time to actively listen to students and help them find ways to decrease stressors in their lives.
- Schedule time to organize. Especially in lower grades, providing time to organize desks and cubbies, sharpen pencils, and put away toys and tools can give students a greater sense of control.
- Encourage students to face their anxieties in baby steps. Come up with techniques that allow them to participate a bit more each time.
- Establish a routine and implement your own time management techniques. A hectic classroom schedule is a common stressor for students.
- Encourage students to perform visualization and breathing activities prior to stressful events, such as games and tests.
- Pay attention to student interactions to prevent bullying and abuse within your classroom.
- Pay attention to behavioral changes in your students. If concerning behaviors are continually exhibited, check your school's policy and reach out to parents, guardians and/or a counselor.
- Provide patience and encouragement.
- Have conversations with your students about failure. It is important for them to understand that everyone fails at things and that when they fail, it does not mean that they are failures.

CHILDREN AND DEPRESSION

Depression is a serious mood disorder that can take the joy from a child's life. It is normal for a child to be moody or sad from time to time. However, if these feelings last more than two weeks, and start to interfere with daily activities, it may be a sign of clinical depression. The following list of symptoms may help you identify if a child is experiencing depression.

- Frequent sadness, or crying more often or more easily
- Poor concentration
- Increased irritability, anger, or hostility
- Hopelessness
- Decreased interest in activities, or an inability to enjoy usual activities
- Persistent boredom or low energy
- Social isolation/withdrawal: Spending more time alone, away from family and friends
- Violence towards self or others
- "Clingy" and more dependent behavior in certain relationships
- Overly pessimistic attitude or excessive guilt
- Feelings of worthlessness and extreme sensitivity to rejection or failure
- Difficulty with relationships
- Over or under eating, or any form of addictive behavior
- Frequent complaints of physical illnesses, such as headaches and stomachaches
- Frequent absences from school or poor performance in school
- Major changes in eating and/or sleeping patterns
- Talk of, or efforts to, run away from home
- Self-destructive behavior or self-harm
- Thoughts of death or expressions of suicide
- Increase in risk-taking behaviors and/or showing less concern for their own safety
- Younger children may act younger than their age (regression)
- Low self-steem

MANAGING DEPRESSION

Depression may look different in a child than in an adult, and therefore many children do not get the treatment they need. If you believe your child may be depressed, it is important to take active steps to get your child the help they need. You can help them manage their depression in the following ways:

AT HOME

- Consult with your child's pediatrician or family physician. A mental health assessment and evaluation can be done for a diagnosis and treatment plan. Your doctor may refer you to a mental health professional such as a psychiatrist, psychologist, or counselor. *(Do not delay treatment. Early detection and diagnosis are important for getting your child the help they need. Though parents can often feel responsible for what is happening with their children, they did not cause the depression.)*
- Respect your child's feelings but don't empower the feelings. It is important to acknowledge that their feelings are real and valid and help them find the source of the anxiety they are feeling. However, once they have acknowledged their anxiety, it is important to help children learn to face their fears. Make sure you are not reinforcing fears with your behaviors.
- Make sure your child is getting proper rest and nutrition. Children need a well-balanced diet and 9-12 hours of sleep each night to stay physically and mentally healthy.
- Life stressors such as an illness, a separation/divorce, a move, or death can trigger short-term problems or lead to depression. Under these stressors, it is helpful for families to turn to a mental health professional. Depression is treatable, but, if left untreated, can be life threatening. Depression is a major risk factor for suicide.
- Communicate with your child's school. Teachers, school psychologists, and social workers are there to help.
- Talk to your child and listen carefully. Never dismiss feelings, but point out realities and offer hope.
- Remind your child that you are always there to help and support them. Depressed children need continual reassurance. It is common for them to feel unworthy when experiencing depression.
- Remind your child that they are important and needed.
- Encourage and be a positive role model for a healthy lifestyle. Getting proper nutrition, having adequate sleep, and exercising all help alleviate stress, build relationships, and improve mood.
- Help your child with problem-solving skills. Develop a plan of realistic steps your child can take toward a goal, recognize their success on the path, and encourage the enjoyment of the experience along the way. Help identify potential obstacles or difficulties and plan/talk about ways to overcome them. Focus on strengths.

- Never ignore statements and comments about death or suicide. Report them to your child's doctor immediately and if you believe your child is in immediate danger do not leave them alone. Contact your local emergency room in the US; or numbers at the end of this document. You may develop a safety and emergency plan of your own. Have a list of numbers ready to call.

AT SCHOOL

- Communicate with the student's parents, as well as the school psychologists and social workers.
- Talk to your student and listen carefully. Never dismiss feelings, but point out realities and offer hope.
- Use positive reinforcement and methods of discipline that promote self-esteem.
- Use frequent "movement" breaks between lessons to keep students active and engaged. Exercise can help decrease depression and increase mindfulness.
- Schedule time to organize. Especially in lower grades, providing time to organize desks and cubbies, sharpen pencils, and put away toys and tools can give students a greater sense of control.
- Establish a routine and implement your own time management techniques. A hectic classroom schedule can be an additional stressful obstacle for students to deal with.
- Remind your student that you are always there to help and support them. Depressed children need continual reassurance. It is common for them to feel unworthy when experiencing depression.
- Help your student with problem-solving skills. Develop a plan of realistic steps your student can take toward an academic goal, recognize their success on the path, and encourage the enjoyment of the experience along the way. Help identify potential obstacles or difficulties and plan/talk about ways to overcome them. Focus on strengths.
- Never ignore statements and comments about death or suicide. Report them to the school counselor and the student's parents immediately. If you believe your student is in immediate danger do not leave them alone. Contact your local emergency room in the US; or numbers at the end of this document. You may develop a safety and emergency plan of your own. Have a list of numbers ready to call.

If a parent notices concerning symptoms in their child, such as changes in mood, behavior, or overall well-being, it's important to reach out to a local healthcare professional. Early guidance and support can make a significant difference in addressing potential mental health concerns and ensuring the child receives the appropriate care.

Additional Resources for Parents

For more information on the challenges to hope, check out the following resources:

- **Hopeful Minds Overview: 3 Lessons, Lesson 3** *(www.hopefulminds.org/hopeful-minds-curriculums/)*
- **CDC: Violence Prevention - Adverse Childhood Experiences** *(https://www.cdc.gov/violenceprevention/childabuseandneglect/acestudy/index.html)*
- **9 Types of Hopelessness and How to Overcome Them** *(https://psychcentral.com/blog/the-9-types-of-hopelessness-and-how-to-overcome-them/)*
- **ACEs Aware** *(https://www.acesaware.org/)*
- **Global Prevalence of Depressive and Anxiety Symptoms in Children and Adolescents During COVID-19** *(https://jamanetwork.com/journals/jamapediatrics/fullarticle/2782796#:~:text=Across%2029%20samples%20and%2080,experiencing%20clinically%20elevated%20anxiety%20symptoms.)*
- **Adverse childhood experiences: a meta-analysis of prevalence and moderators among half a million adults in 206 studies** *(https://onlinelibrary.wiley.com/doi/10.1002/wps.21122)*

For more information on neutralizing negative feelings in your life and your children's lives, check out these additional resources:

- **Hopeful Minds Overview: 3 Lesson Curriculum, Lesson 2** *(www.hopefulminds.org/hopeful-minds-curriculums/)*
- **The 90-Second Rule You Can't Afford to Ignore** *(https://onebodyinc.com/the-90-second-rule-you-cant-afford-to-ignore/)*
- **8 Yoga Poses for Stress Relief for Kids** *(https://gozen.com/8-yoga-poses-for-stress-relief-for-kids/)*
- **Researchers Find Out Why Some Stress is Good for You** *(http://news.berkeley.edu/2013/04/16/researchers-find-out-why-some-stress-is-good-for-you/)*

For more information on fostering positive feelings in your life and your children's lives, check out these additional resources:

- **Hopeful Minds Overview: 3 Lesson Curriculum, Lesson 2** *(www.hopefulminds.org/hopeful-minds-curriculums/)*
- **The Neuroanatomical Transformation of the Teenage Brain: Jill Bolte Taylor** *(https://www.youtube.com/watch?v=PzT_SBl31-s)*
- **Experiencing and Expressing Emotion** *(https://counselingcenter.illinois.edu/brochures/experiencing-and-expressing-emotion)*

For additional resources on SMART Goal-Setting, check out:

- **Hopeful Minds Overview: 3 Lesson Curriculum, Lesson 2** *(https://hopefulminds.org/hopeful-minds-curriculums/)*
- **SMART Goals: How to Make Your Goals Achievable** *(https://www.mindtools.com/pages/article/smart-goals.htm)*
- **Achieving Your Goals: An Evidence-Based Approach** *(https://www.canr.msu.edu/news/achieving_your_goals_an_evidence_based_approach)*

OTHER RESOURCES

- **Autism Speaks** *(https://www.autismspeaks.org/resource-guide)*
- **Children and Adults with Attention-Deficit/Hyperactivity Disorder (CHADD)** *(https://chadd.org/)*
- **Explaining the Brain to Children and Adolescents** *(https://vimeo.com/109042767)*
- **Heart Rate Variability: A New Way to Track Well-Being** *(https://www.health.harvard.edu/blog/heart-rate-variability-new-way-track-well-2017112212789)*
- **International Therapist Directory** *(https://internationaltherapistdirectory.com/)*
- **Gain Hope: A Place for Hope in the Age of Anxiety** *(http://www.gainhope.com/hope/default.cfm)*
- **Fight, Flight, Freeze Responses** *(https://trauma-recovery.ca/impact-effects-of-trauma/fight-flight-freeze-responses/)*

Hope Journey: Next Steps

Ready to teach your children about hope, and implement Stress Skills and Happiness Habits in your home? Our 3 lesson curriculum and 16 lesson curriculum help introduce children to hope in easy-to-understand ways, and provide hands-on worksheets and activities.

Hopeful Minds currently offers three sets of lessons for elementary school students:

Hopeful Minds Overview Curriculum

Hopeful Minds Deep Dive Curriculum

Hopeful Minds Teen Hopeguide

ADDITIONAL COURSE OFFERINGS

Hopeful Mindsets Deep Dive College

Hopeful Mindsets Overview

Hopeful Mindsets Workplace Overview

Hopeful Mindsets for Veterans

All Hopeful Minds lessons and resources can be accessed at www.hopefulminds.org/curriculums. If you would like to be notified when new curriculum and resources become available, or if you have questions or feedback, please reach out to us at activate@theshinehopecompany.com.

Where to Find Support

U.S. SUICIDE HOTLINES AND IMMEDIATE TELEPHONE SUPPORT

If you or someone you know needs immediate help in the U.S., call any of the lines for hope below to talk to someone in your local area. They can listen to you and direct you to local resources if further assistance is needed. If someone has talked to you about suicide, and you believe they are currently a threat to themselves or someone else but won't take your help, call 911.

988	United States Crisis Hotline. *Hours: Available 24 hours. Languages: English, Spanish.*
(888)628-9454	National Suicide Prevention Lifeline: *Spanish Language Available*
(800)799-4889	National Suicide Prevention Lifeline: *Deaf & Hard of Hearing Options*
(800)784-2432	1-800-SUICIDA Spanish Speaking Suicide Hotline
(877)968-8454	1-877-YOUTHLINE Teen to Teen Peer Counseling Hotline
(866)488-7386	TrevorLifeLine for LGBTQ Support
(877)565-8860	Trans Lifeline

You can also text HOME to 741741 to connect with a crisis counselor from crisistextline.org.

TO FIND A LIST OF INTERNATIONAL RESOURCES VISIT https://findahelpline.com/i/iasp or Scan the QR Code:

If you are in need of support, you can find additional resources by visiting www.theshinehopecompany.com/get-support/ or scanning the QR Code.

www.ingramcontent.com/pod-product-compliance
Lightning Source LLC
Chambersburg PA
CBHW081510080526
44589CB00017B/2721